T0131533

Four Lessons
of
Psychoanalysis

Four Lessons of Psychoanalysis

Moustafa Safouan

Edited by
Anna Shane

Other Press
New York

Copyright © 2004 Moustafa Safouan

Production Editor: Robert D. Hack

This book was set in 11 pt. Berkeley by Alpha Graphics of Pittsfield, New Hampshire.

ISBN-13: 978-1-59051-087-2

All rights reserved. No part of this publication may be reproduced or transmitted in any form or by any means, electronic or mechanical, including photocopying, recording, or by any information storage and retrieval system, without written permission from Other Press LLC, except in the case of brief quotations in reviews for inclusion in a magazine, newspaper, or broadcast. Printed in the United States of America on acid-free paper. For information write to Other Press LLC, 2 Park Avenue, 24th Floor, New York, NY 10016. Or visit our Web site: www.otherpress.com.

ISBN-13: 978-1-59051-087-2

Library of Congress Cataloging-in-Publication Data

Safouan, Moustafa.
  Four lessons of psychoanalysis / by Moustafa Safouan ; edited by Anna Shane.
    p. cm.
  ISBN 1-59051-087-9 (pbk. : alk. paper)
  1. Psychoanalysis. 2. Lacan, Jacques, 1901- 3. Freud, Sigmund, 1856–1939. I. Shane, Anna. II. Title.
  BF175 .S19 2004
  150.19'5–dc22

                                        2003022344

Contents

I wish to acknowledge the contributions of Anna Shane to the production of *Four Lessons of Psychoanalysis*. It would never have seen the light of day without her commitment. It is a work of interlocution and she was my interlocutor.

—Moustafa Safouan, July 2002

1

I think the best way to begin would be to tell you my conception of the work to be done during this week and if you see points I've omitted, or if there are others you wish to add, you may make suggestions. My plan can be adapted to your suggestions.

I think Freud's work culminates in a theory that contains a certain number of contradictions. If any one of them remains unanswered, it would be enough to ruin the theory or be considered a refutation of it. I'll limit myself to reminding you of the two most well-known contradictions. Transference is considered the condition sine qua non of psychoanalysis, so much so that analysis came to be considered analysis of the transference. Yet transference is also considered to be the most powerful obstacle to its progress. So, how can transference be both a condition of possibility *and* a factor of impossibility? The other contradiction concerns the ego. Freud began by defining the ego as a reality function, and this was very important to him as far as desires were concerned. Desires tend, according to Freud, to the hallucination of their objects, meaning they find their satisfactions in objects that have nothing to do with reality. Without a reality function to correct the function of desire, the psychic function would be reduced to hallucination, to psychotic states. With the discovery of narcissism, however, the ego was next envisioned as the agent that makes me mistake what I am for what I want to be. So how can the same agent be both a guide to reality *and* a source of illusion?

In addition to these two contradictions in his theory, Freud's experience led him to discover some astonishing facts, so astonishing you may say they qualify as unnatural, so their explanation is not easy to find. I allude here to the castration complex. How does it happen that the boy feels insecure about his penis? Where does the threat of castration come from? At the same time, how does it happen that the girl may feel a lack of a penis, which is as reasonable as someone feeling the lack of a third eye, or of a sixth sense?

And there is also the fact that psychoanalytic experience led to the discovery of two different phenomena. First there is the phenomenon of love transference, characterized by idealization. Actually, idealization is the essence of all love. The object of love is seen as a whole, not only in the sense of unity or totality but also in the sense of having all that I lack. On the other hand, we notice in the same experience a number of desires, each one of them valorized by what you may call a partial object—oral, anal, you may add the gaze and the voice, but the main point is their character as partial objects. So you don't easily see the relation between the two phenomena—between love and desire, or in other words, between the total and the partial object.

To my knowledge Jacques Lacan is the only analyst who has made an assiduous and consistent effort to meet the whole range of these problems, and what I think of doing during this week is giving you the answers that an analyst who takes Lacan's work into consideration may give to these problems. Do you agree with this idea?

The first point is that, in his work, Lacan referred to a completely new definition of the psychoanalytic experience itself; he defined it as an experience of discourse. His formula, "the unconscious is structured as language," has been repeated so often that now it seems obvious. But before Lacan analysts analyzed other things, for example personality or the dynamics of the unconscious, and speech itself was considered to be something that had no value unless it expressed some "reality" or other. Of course there was the definition of psychoanalysis as a talking therapy, but once again, the talking was considered to be an expression of some reality outside the talking. Before Lacan no one thought of locating the subject *within the very act of talking*.

You can find the idea of psychoanalysis being a matter of speech, however, in Freud's *Studies on Hysteria*.[1] In the final chapter, "Psychotherapy of Hysteria," Freud devotes three or four pages to the description of what he calls the disposition of psychic material in what is *said* during a psychoanalytic session. He says that discourse should be represented not by one single line but by many parallel lines:

_____

_____

_____

_____

_____

that is, like a musical notation. These lines are supposed to represent many themes, such as dreams, memories, descriptions of feelings or emotions, and words that are sometimes acts, according to Austin's idea, for instance an apology or a demand. The concrete discourse that is uttered by the analysand, however, can't be represented simply by these straight lines, because someone may start saying something about a memory, and while talking about that memory she thinks of a dream, which makes her think of a linguistic expression, which makes her feel a bodily symptom. So the concrete discourse

1. Freud, S. *Standard Edition* 2:288–292.

should be represented by a zigzag movement, which Freud compares to the movements of the horse in a game of chess.

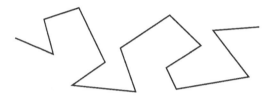

Of course, one line would hardly be sufficient to give a full picture of a real discourse, because someone may start with a fantasy, then go to a dream, then to a linguistic expression, and then to a demand or an apology, and so on. So if you want a fuller picture of what goes on in a session, you must have many zigzag lines that cross each other. And, of course no scheme can really give a picture of the structure of a discourse. But the main thing is, according to Freud, the lines of discourse tend to meet up at the same point. The discourse is apparently free, which is to say that it is a discourse maintained without a special end in view. But psychoanalytic experience proves that it is subtended by a kind of blind *intentionality*, which unknowingly directs it toward a *pathogenic nucleus*. This nucleus is surrounded by what Freud's describes as layers of memories, going from the most recent to the most ancient, so you may represent them by circles like this, circles of memory:

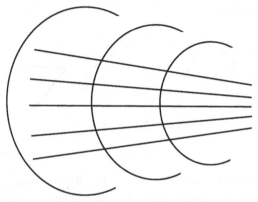

The decisive point is that, according to Freud, as the lines of discourse move unknowingly toward the pathogenic nucleus, they encounter other, vertical lines, which represent resistance:

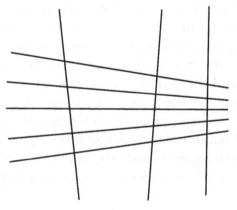

This means that in the measure that the discourse advances on its path, you will come across the phenomenon of resistance. The most familiar example of this phenomenon is that the analysand suddenly becomes aware of your presence saying, "Oh, I feel you are here," or "I wonder if you are still in the room," or "I wonder if you're listening," or she thinks about the surroundings. So what does this mean?

According to Lacan, this means that in the very measure in which the discourse is about to exercise *its function as a revelation*, the ego manifests itself as included in a relation of you and me. So the ego, whose intervention in the discourse is represented by the vertical lines, is the main agent of resistance. This goes in the direction of considering the ego as antagonistic to the revelation of what you may call the truth.

Insofar as Lacan adhered to this representation of the movement of discourse in the psychoanalytic session and insofar as he defined the ego as an agent of resistance to the progress of the discourse, by the same token he adhered to the conception of the ego as a narcissistic agent. And so, Lacan resolved the contradiction between Freud's two conceptions of the ego by choosing one of the alternatives: he chose to define the ego as a narcissistic object and not as a function of reality. Why was he inclined to choose this alternative? There are some points you may consider to be invariables in Lacan's thought.

The first point is that Lacan was always convinced that the human object cannot be identified with the object of knowledge. To him the idea of an object of knowledge is the result of a long tradition of occidental thought. For Lacan there is another, more primitive object: the object of desire. He had reasons for his conviction. First he was a psychiatrist, so he had the experience of an object of anxiety or depersonalization or strangeness, or states like déjà vu. That's an object you don't master as you might master your computer, or your fork and spoon, or any other common object. It's rather an object that leaves you disarmed. And even in our everyday experience desire is most often experienced as regret or nostalgia, or it is defined as "that which I don't know," or "I didn't mean that," or "I don't know what I want," or "I wanted something else." So you can even say that the object of desire as commonly experienced is always the Other thing.

And from this point of view it is not astonishing that Lacan came to have some affinity with Hegel. Of course, Hegel was the last philosopher to contest the status of the object as something other than an object of knowledge. But he was the first one to represent the object of desire, not as a natural object, but as an object mediated by the other: for Hegel what man wants is what the other has. Of course, this is also a very common experience. The child psychologists discovered it as a state characteristic of children of a certain age, between 18 months and 3 years: They called it transidivism. You might see a little girl looking at another girl eating some chocolate, and then she hits her. When asked why, she claims it was the other one who hit *her*, and she isn't lying. There is a fundamental ambiguity that makes for her logic: what she gives is lived by her as if it were received, like a relation with a mirror.

This means there is some ambiguity concerning how an action is lived: at the same time activity is lived as passivity and passivity is lived as activity. The one who parades sees herself in the other's eyes, living it as if she herself is over there, in the eyes of the other one who watches her. You may say that here the ego fundamentally mistakes itself, finds itself where it is not, or in two places at the same time. So this was at least a first approach to desire, not as natural, not as related to a real lack, such as thirst to water or hunger to food. The most serious example of this kind of misrecognition is what Hegel called the "beautiful soul," a description of the position of the subject who denounces the disorder of the world rather than acknowledging her own disorder. For the beautiful soul denunciation is the means of misrecognizing her own disorder. This corresponds to what is called projection, but we see that the very root of projection is related to the alienated structure of the ego. Lacan's doctoral thesis concerned a case of a woman who had many ambitions about herself as a writer, and who developed an imaginary relation to a well-known actress as her ideal ego. As can be expected in such relations, she had to find an outlet in some act. Indeed, it finished in an act of aggression, which led to this woman being hospitalized. This case was an example of the beautiful soul described by Hegel.

But then you may ask: If the ego is defined by narcissism, or if there is no reality function, then why aren't we all psychotics or beautiful souls? The answer is that what is at stake in psychoanalysis is not reality, but truth. Insofar as we perceive with our senses, a psychotic is as well equipped as we. But psychoanalysis is not about sense reality, it's about truth, which is a very different matter. Moreover, if the ego is an agent of misrecognition, then there must then be *someone* who knows the truth in order to rectify a relation to it. And so, if we go back to the scheme of resistance, we are led to a new technique in interpreting: If resistance is a function of the progress of the analysand's discourse, that is, a function of its proximity to truth, then you won't need to tell your analysand, for example, that she's resisting your interpretation. You would do better to tell her that her symptom intensified (a fact Freud considered as a proof that the symptom has its own say) or that her ideas were interrupted, at the very place she was speaking about this or that topic.

When Lacan first proposed this way of handling resistance, it was very difficult for practicing analysts to take in. That's because an analyst's prestige comes from her conviction that *she* knows the truth, and that she's the one who's going to tell it to the analysand. Lacan's way means that you can't identify with such a position, that you have to abdicate it. This wasn't easy for analysts, so at first his thesis was not as readily admitted as it now may be.

This brings up the question of the place of truth. When you hear a lapsus that betrays some truth,[2] you can't say that this truth dwells in you (because you noticed it), or even that it has its home in the subject (whose signifiers betrayed it). It would be more descriptively adequate to say that its place is that of the Other, with a capital O, because here it is a matter of a different kind of otherness, which has nothing to do with vision and nothing to do with the image or semblance, but which has everything to do with language and the talking subject. This was another of the points that were difficult to assimilate, but you can see that these points go together. Once you consider psychoanalysis as a talking therapy without trying to go outside the talking, then you have to describe the ego as an agent of resistance. And once you subscribe to the narcissistic

2. Editor's note: see p. 79.

definition of the ego, you will have to realize that what you are concerned with in the talking is not reality, but truth. And then you'll have to admit that truth is not a possession of the ego, but that truth dwells in some Other place.

From here we can go to another point, which is that if rectification is not the analyst's work, and if truth signifies itself not in the ego but in, for instance, wit or lapsus or acting out or things like that, then this fact of signification of what is true (or of what is false, the appearance of one being equivalent to the appearance of the other) would be impossible if language consisted of units, the so-called signifiers, and if each of them had only one meaning. I mean that if words were tied to their denotations, if they were clean of all equivocation, that is, if they were liable to no ambiguity, then there would be no liberty in signifying the true while saying something false. For example, take wit: you can say a word that apparently has a common meaning but use it in such a way that the listener hears a different meaning, one that wasn't at all expected. This is what gives truth the capacity to express itself, independent of our intentions. This capacity depends on the independence of the signifier regarding signification.

And, this is the meaning of the famous representation by Saussure, when he writes it like this[3]:

3. Editor's note: This is a simplification of Saussure's notation.

tree   S

You have the (S)ignifier (tree) and the (s)ignification, which is the tree itself, written with a line between them, which is generally read as the line of their union. But for Lacan it's a line of separation, it expresses *the distinction* between the two planes. Although the two planes are separate, however, this doesn't mean there is no relation between them. There is a relation, not the relation of the tree calling for a word, but rather the word that, in its different uses, may determine different significations.

But signification in language is a function of phrases, not of words. For a logician like Gottlob Frege the meaning of a phrase is the outcome of the addition of the meanings of the words. But according to I. A. Richards, the rhetorician, the meaning of the phrase is given only when you reach the end of the phrase; only then can you understand the beginning. At the end of the phrase each element within the composition gets its meaning in a retroactive movement. This is the same idea Lacan advocates. On this point he agrees with rhetoricians like Richards, and not with logicians like Frege.

The point is that this relation, understood as a crossing of the line of separation between signifier and signified, added to the fact that truth always comes by way of surprise, may indicate another kind of resistance than the one that is simply the resistance of the ego. There may be a resistance in the sense of some inherent difficulty in telling the truth. Truth is not something that can be said bluntly. Truth always signifies itself, not in a straightforward way, but indirectly and in a way that surprises. And here you may ask, the truth of what?

Considering all that we have said up until now, the answer will leave no doubt: it is the truth of unconscious desire. And the difficulty alluded to is that it is the nature of such desire to consist in what Lacan calls *mi-dire*. That is, it can only be signified by way of allusion. What can we now say about unconscious desire? This is a question I'll leave for the next session. For the moment I hope I've clarified its relation with the signifier as such. If something is not yet clear, we'll deal with it in answering the questions.

Question: I'm amazed, Mr. Safouan, that you always go back to Freud, and recap what seems to Lacanians as basic but refreshing. You capture the problem of the ego, getting this by an old book by Freud that isn't referred to any more, and you refer again to Saussure and the bar, and how this is, in the clinic. It seems new again. I'm not adding anything to what you said.

I'm sorry I didn't have time to find the exact pages where Freud gives this description of the disposition of psychic material in the discourse, but you'll find it in the final chapter of the *Studies on Hysteria*. As far as your remarks are concerned, I would add that the contradictions I've alluded to are the kinds of contradictions one feels at the beginning of one's practice: How can the ego be both an instance of misrecognition and a reality function? How can transference be both a condition for psychoanalytic work and an obstacle to it? In my own experience, for example, I happened to have a patient who had never seen his father, his father having left him when he was less than 3 years old. But in spite of that, all the material he gave pointed to a very strong superego; his actions had an auto-punitive character, he was prone to accidents, he suffered from every kind of imperative, and all the symbols in his dreams pointed to the severity of this instance. According to the theory, however, the superego was an inheritance from the father. So how could this analysand have such a severe superego when his father had disappeared when he was so young? One couldn't go on working with the accumulation of such paradoxes and contradictions. But when Lacan introduced the distinction between the real, imaginary, and symbolic father, it gave one hope that there may be a solution.

That's why there was transference onto Lacan; he gave his students the promise of a consistent knowledge. It was a credit given to him. Of course, a credit isn't a belief, it's something more like a confidence, one you will have to test. I say this as an echo to your remark, to underline that from the beginning the relation with Lacan was a relation to an analyst who had made it his job to answer the problems that were left in Freud's work. Analysts who didn't start out with Lacan don't always see these connections, because his discourse led to the introduction of new signifiers and created some new problems, which took over their attention.

Question: What are these new problems?

There aren't contradictions but there are serious problems. For example, take the object of desire named the *obj. a* in its relation to representation. Does this object exist outside all representation or can it exist as a representation? The word "representation" has more than one meaning. There can be, for instance, a representation of representation, as in the painting of Velázquez in which he represents himself in the act of representation. This painting is itself a representation. But does the object of desire exist on that level? This is a difficult problem to tackle and Lacan was never clear about it. There are also other problems we are going to consider, although in my opinion they aren't actually contradictions; I would rather speak about obscurities and difficulties. As far as desire is concerned, it's clear that it represents a kind of lack that is different from the lack of need. A desire is not the same thing as a need, and consequently its object is not an object to have, as is the case with objects of need. We are led, therefore, to talk about a lack at the level of *being*. And here intervenes the notion of castration with its complexities.

Question: This notion of being, what does Lacan refer to? To me it seems that his notion of being is not always used in the same way.

It is because there is a lack of being that there is idealization. Moreover, there are some other strange phenomena, like feeling the penis as a lack. This is a lack that can't be understood on the level of having; you have to introduce the dimension of being. The question is, what form does the lack take, and how is it introduced? This problem depends on a wide range of correlative problems.

Question: But would you trace the notion of being away from phenomenology, to Lacan's own use of being?

The notion of being is related to the notion of one-ness, and the notion of oneness is related to the very fact that you may make what you call a trait, but if you make a trait you must have another trait. By definition, a trait is repetitive. Here you have a point where difference is the same as sameness and sameness the same as difference, which is the definition of the signifier. So, the notion of being is rather to be explained by the notion of the oneness of the trait, as giving its own structure to the signifier as defined by its own difference. All this we'll have to look at more closely, but the point is, it's related not to a phenomenon but to the structure of the signifier as difference.

Question: You don't use an essentialist definition?

No. When a primitive man sees a rat and says, "This is my dead master who has come back as a rat," on the qualitative level there is no sameness. Qualitatively these are two completely different things; one can only say they're the same because it's a matter of manipulating or articulating signifiers, and it is on that level that sameness is the definition of difference, and difference the definition of sameness. Wherever there is talk about being, you'll find that it is a talk about sameness. And the talk about sameness postulates talk about difference. One has to coordinate these three points together.

Question: Is there time now to say something about ethics?

We'll have time later, but right now we may point out that talk about the desire of the analyst isn't a talk about metaphysics, it concerns real institutional problems. An Englishman sent a letter to *The London Review of Books*[4] that was supposedly a description of his "analysis" with Masud Khan. But it was simply a description of a man being exploited by another man in the most callous way. Of course, publication of this letter brought many reactions. There was, for example, the response from the head of the British society, who pointed out that Khan had mismanaged the treatment because at the end of his life he'd suffered from some disequilibria, but that the patient in question had undergone a second analysis, in the United States, which had had excellent results, so all's well that ends well. Another reader, who was the president of a society that covers the psychotherapeutic business in England, wrote to the effect that

4. *London Review of Books*, Vol. 23, No. 4, Februry 22, 2001, by Wayne Godley.

these things will sometimes happen, but there is a full investigation underway, and they are now writing new rules to check this kind of abuse from ever happening again. A third man, who was not an analyst, wrote, "I wonder why every time something like this happens you defend psychoanalysis, at any cost? Why don't you just admit that the analysis was a failure?"

Lacan's position is somehow akin to that of the third man. But here there is an important difference between Lacan on the one hand, and Thomas Szasz and Ida Macalpine on the other. Szasz wouldn't see it as accidental abuse resulting from countertransference but as something inherent in the psychoanalytic situation, because the psychoanalytic situation puts the patient in a state of subjugation and liability to suggestion. Consequently, Szasz quit the field of psychoanalysis, and so did Macalpine. This is nothing like Lacan's position. Lacan asked, why even make a claim of countertransference? If there is analysis, it's supposed to introduce a change in the libidinal economy. Since libido means the energy of desire, a didactic analysis is supposed to lead to a libidinal modification that brings out a desire more powerful than, for example, the desire to take your patient into your arms, not to mention the desire to exploit her! For Lacan the notion of countertransference was simply an alibi to avoid looking more clearly at the kind of modification of libidinal economy that prepares one to be an analyst. So the question of the desire of the analyst came to the forefront of Lacan's teaching as a result of his critique of the notion of countertransference. (And it's obviously also a very different point of view than simply calling for the rescue of the law.) This shows that Lacan's reflection on the matter of ethics, considered as the ethics of desire, started from serious problems, which analytic institutions had done their best to dodge.

Question: But Lacan's answer didn't seem to work either!

You can't say that an analyst's desire is a desire for this or that, but when we study the varieties of lack (and there are at least three varieties—privation, frustration, and castration), thanks to Lacan we can at least situate the analyst's desire in a register of lack. I spoke about the mediated character of desire in Hegel, but I also pointed out that there is another kind of mediation, because we found another kind of Other, not just another fellow, the small other. The distinction between the two introduces another kind of mediation. You can't say what the object of desire *is*, but you can, say, assign it to a register of lack. So here is at least a workable contribution.

Question: Can you say the source of the problem is the gap between what institutions are and the practice of psychoanalysis, that the tendency of institutions creates the crisis, by claiming they have something to offer?

That's Lacan's whole point in doing away with the idea of grades. He didn't use grades, and instead introduced the idea of the passage, which takes place during analysis, and refers to the subject, inasmuch as the subject has to be located within her discourse, within speech. This idea of the subject is completely alien to institutions, as much as it is to human sciences. The one who enters an institution wants a career, which implies an ideal, a chief, and the one whose place she will one day take. In all institutions a need for anticipation and ideals leads to hierarchies, and to the idea of the grade.

What did Lacan want to do and why did his own institution fail? What is the significance of this failure? These are questions of another kind, which we may have some occasion to deal with. But the idea was to make an institution without grades and without a hierarchy. Inasmuch as there will be some result from an analysis, the result will be acknowledged not by a master, but by a study of what happened within the analysis, of the analysis itself.

What is the result of an analysis? The main point you have to consider is that the criterion of efficacy asks the question, "Is analysis capable of stopping repetition or isn't it?" At the same time, since Freud says that repetition is characteristic of all drives, if you make repetition cease, will you then put an end to the drives? What is the destiny of the drives after analysis? What, for instance, happens to your gregarious instinct? Does it still find its satisfaction in belonging to a political party? What do your children mean to you when they are no longer your *objs. a*? What is the destiny of the drives after analysis, or even within analysis? Outcome then depends on what you learn from an analysand herself concerning the modification of her own libidinal economy. That was the point of introducing the passage (*la passe*) in place of the grade.

Question: Lacan didn't answer what the fate of the drive is after analysis.

No. The point of the experience called *la passe* was to throw some light onto this question of the outcome of the analysis concerning drives.

Question: To return to something quite well known, have you acted in accordance with your desire? Every desire needs to reshape its goal, so every desire *is* its interpretation. So the ethics of analysis concerns the question: Have you kept on interpreting what you want? Isn't this the real ethics of analysis? It's a must to always find a new interpretation, because one can never name the object of love or hate.

The idea of desire as interpretation comes as a consequence of another kind of mediation, when the other is small. The other may have a bar of chocolate, or a house, or a girlfriend, and this is enough to make you desire the same thing she has; this is the Hegelian mediation. When she is defined, however, not as another ego but as another *subject*, her desire escapes you. Whatever she may say, you can never be sure she's telling the truth. There is always a question of *why* she's saying this or that, and if you define her desire by giving it an interpretation, you have it at your mercy. In this way desire is an interpretation of the Other's desire.

You may sometimes hear an analysand using metaphors, such as to "rob," or "spoil," or "devour." These kinds of metaphors may give you an idea about the oral character of her interpretation of the Other's desire. But if you tell her this "interpretation" of the Other's desire, the Other then loses its authenticity, for the benefit of what you may call a paranoid knowledge and a certitude. It is from your interpretation of the Other's desire that you draw your certitude: You are *sure* what the Other wants of you. This is the first position of desire, and it's not easy to get out of this position, with all the certitude that it implies. We can see an example of the main point in dreams. A dream satisfies a desire in the sense of a fantasy. But the question is, what is the desire is outside the dream: to stay in the fantasy or to traverse the fantasy?[5] That's the point. A dream may fulfill a desire, in the sense of fulfilling a fantasy, but a fantasy is also a

5. Editor's note: see pp. 58, 68, 73, 81.

burden. Although a fantasy has the advantage of giving you certitudes, it's also a burden, at the very least the burden of imagining that the Other to whom you attribute an oral desire wants to devour you. So it's a source of certitude but it's also a source of the anxiety of its being realized.

You may even say (with a grain of salt) that desire is knowledge, inasmuch as it is interpretation, but it's a knowledge one is ethically required to give up, because it's also a misrecognition, insofar as *any* interpretation of the Other's desire makes the Other lose its authenticity, as unknown.

Question: Would you please elaborate?

You can say indeed that desire is an interpretation, but *as* an interpretation it gives you a false certitude of what the Other desires of you. It gives you a kind of knowledge, but a kind that deserves to be described as paranoid. For example, when you look at the relation between desire and the dream, the dream realizes desire in the sense of granting you your wish: your desire is to kill your brother and you may realize this wish in a dream where he appears as dead. But outside the dream, is it your desire to kill your brother or to be rid of the desire to kill him? That's the whole point! As far as ethics comes in, you may say that the subject is ethically required to restore to the Other its very dimension of being unknown, that is, to escape all transparency that the mirror may give to you. In other words, you may say that the subject is required to stop all pretension to knowledge as far as the Other is concerned.

Question: There is a misreading of "do not give up on your desire," as "do not give up your demands."

Yes, of course. The whole neurotic position is based on the confusion between desire and demand. When you ask the question, "What does the Other want of me?" the fact of any answer at all implies an assimilation of desire to demand. This is a point that will be explained when we speak about how Lacan arrived at the difference between desire and demand.

Question: Is an ethics of the drive possible?

The point is to have analysts who don't pretend to know the unconscious. They may hear the *half-said*, but only later; they don't pretend to know in advance. The analysand comes to you as if you're someone who knows what's in her unconscious. The analyst accepts this, but knows it's a misunderstanding. The analyst has to help the analysand escape this misunderstanding.[6] It's a point

6. Editor's note: See pp. 60, 66, 68.

of assuming a certain amount of structural ignorance concerning this Other.

Question: I have a question about anxiety. It's something I've struggled with before: the difference between a *passage à l'acte*, acting out and the analytic act. Would you like to comment?

These questions will be dealt with later. But by way of anticipation, as far as acting out and *passage à l'acte*, the best example is in Freud's case of the homosexual girl,[7] the girl who made a homosexual choice after having been disappointed by the fact that her father didn't give her what she was expecting from him. (A brother was born and after his birth she turned to the homosexual trend.) She had a homosexual attachment in a very idealizing vein, meaning she was chivalrous about it. You can consider the whole story with the "lady" she adored as an acting out, inasmuch as it was a process meant to carry a kind of message to her father. You may consider acting out as *going into* the scene of the imaginary in order to signify something. Thus, it calls for interpretation. But when her father failed to understand anything, and was even furious about her liaison (she saw his disapproval in the way he looked at her), she

7. *Standard Edition* 18:145.

then made a suicidal act, jumping *out of* the scene, which was a *passage à l'acte*.

What is characteristic of acting out is going into the scene to signify something. *Passage à l'acte* is throwing oneself outside the scene. This is sufficient to locate the ideas.

Question: A *passage à l'acte* happens when signification fails?

When a signification is not heard in spite of the insistence of the signifier, the outcome is negative transference. When the analysand acts to this deafness by leaving analysis, this is *passage à l'acte*.

Question: Freud says in this example that it also means to get pregnant. Wouldn't you interpret that for her?

An interpretation is a function of what is said *in the moment*.

Question: What would be the analytic act in response to a *passage à l'acte*?

Do you mean when a *passage à l'acte* takes place within analysis?

Question: I mean in Freud's case.

With the homosexual girl? With this girl he himself interrupted her analysis, but that had nothing to do with her *passage à l'acte*, with her jump off the railway bridge. The girl began her analysis with him after that story had finished. After it happened, her father sent her to Freud to, so to speak, make a heterosexual out of her. She started her analysis by reporting dreams the manifest content of which revolved around the theme of heterosexual love and married life. Freud guessed it was all lies, and that her dreams were only meant to deceive him, and he saw only this intention in her dreams. So, instead of asking her why she wanted to deceive him, he interrupted the analysis, which was an astonishing act on his part. In this example, you may say it was Freud who made the *passage à l'acte*.

2

Yesterday the main point of my seminar was, if you consider psychoanalysis as a talking therapy and if instead of going out of the talking to find out what it denotes, you stay within the talking, you situate the subject within the talking act, then you are led to a different conception of otherness than that of the other ego, or what Lacan calls the small other. You are instead led to a conception of otherness as the place of truth, the truth you don't want to know, and as the place of language, the language whose signifiers betray the truth anyway. What I want to deal with today is the question, What is there in this place of the Other? This is the same question as, What is there that remains outside? Or, What is in my relation to language when I say, for example, "I was wrong to treat John the way I did," or "Those years were the best years of my life"? The question is, in other words, What is in my relation to language that remains rebellious to mere reflection?

I would like to approach this subject by first examining the meanings of the word *symbol* in the French school of sociology. Emile Durkheim, the founder of this school, wrote a book entitled *The Rules of the Sociological Method*, and his first axiom was that social facts are things. Around the same time he wrote another book entitled *Elementary Forms of Religion*, in which he considered religion to be the fundamental social tie, that is, the tie that makes for our "togetherness," as members of the same society.

He used the word *symbol* with two nearly opposite meanings. According to the first one, symbol is used as a term in which society takes consciousness of itself. His second meaning was that the symbol is constitutive of society itself. For example, you can consider the symbol "God" as a term in which society takes consciousness of itself as such, of its own unity, that is, as something different from the members of which it is composed since, after all, individuals die while the group as such remains. But you can also consider the same symbol "God" as a condition for the constitution of society, or the social order. I think both uses are worth retaining because many sociologists continue to use the word *symbol* as if it were merely synonymous with representation, that is, as something that stands for something else, which would mean that the word *symbol* covers everything from traffic lights to the rights of man.

Durkheim's disciple and nephew Marcel Mauss was rather dismissive of his second meaning, even though Mauss shared in his uncle's preoccupation with the sacred, with religious phenomena. But besides considering social facts as things, Mauss had a keen feeling for what he called the "total social fact," that is, the fact that constitutes the essence of human society as such. Indeed he grasped this "fact"; he found it in the phenomenon of the gift, inasmuch as it creates the obligation for a return gift.

Then came Claude Levi-Strauss, who took over this idea of gift and countergift, which means exchange. For him exchange was the soul of social existence. The fundamental fact of exchange is, according to him, the exchange of women by men, that is, the laws of marriage. (Here I may say that Levi-Strauss was well aware that laws of marriage may be considered as laws of exchange of men, and that an andocentric view isn't necessary. He adopted the masculine point of view because men held political power in societies, which brought out so many exceptions and anomalies, it made it easier for him to formulate the laws of marriage the way he did.)

But even though laws of marriage differ widely in different societies, one fact remains common to all: the interdiction of incest between mother and son.[1] This means a society may give its king the right to marry his

---

1. Editor's note: see p. 84.

sister, a right that wouldn't be given to anyone else, but that not even a king may marry his mother. Even so, Levi-Strauss considered the law of prohibition of incest to be only a consequence of the main fact, the social fact of exchange, since there would be no exchange if men kept the women for themselves. Thus, what was to be explained was exchange per se, which for him constituted the point of passage from the animal order, the "wild" population, to the cultural order, which is submitted to law. This means he took the idea of exchange to be the total social fact and he eliminated all preoccupation with religious order.

My thesis is that the problem of the passage from the order of nature to that of culture is exactly the same as that of the sacred, and if Levi-Strauss succeeded in eliminating the problem of the sacred, it was because he failed in explaining the exchange. Indeed, his idea was that society has a dual structure, which means that society is composed of an infinite number of pairs or couples, that is, of you's and me's. His point was that this dual relation between two egos makes pacific existence impossible. So, in order to ensure pacific existence, a synthesis must come about, which for him was the exchange. Thus, society proceeded to exchange, in the first place to the exchange of women.

His thesis, however, amounts to saying that it was society that created the condition that makes society.

There is a clear circle in this reasoning. Moreover you can realize that, when you examine the example he gives to illustrate his thought, there is something else at stake. He writes two or three very beautiful pages describing what happens in some country restaurant when two strangers find themselves sitting at the same table, face to face. Each feels embarrassed, an embarrassment that has no other reason than the fact of the presence of another. To put an end to the tension, one offers a taste of his wine to the other one. Then they start to talk and everything is fine. Of course the other fellow asks the first one to taste his wine as well, an exchange that entails no profit for either. The incentive, according to Levi-Strauss, was to pacify the relation in order to make coexistence possible. But if you try to imagine this exchange taking place in silence, as a pantomime, you will then realize that the real exchange that was pacifying was not exchanging wine but was exchanging speech. The exchange of wine was only a celebration of the exchange of speech.

As a matter of fact, one could say that primitive peoples had a keener sense of what is at stake here, because they invented myths of origin that always attributed the creation of the social order, if not existence itself, to the work of some third being that was not a member of their society. Call it the ancestors, the gods, the souls, or whatever it may be; it is this "thirdness" that makes the pair. It is heterogeneous in the sense that, as far as you and I are concerned, we can cheat each other, but the third entity is above all cheating. It is the "witness" and its word is never liable to any falsity.

You may consider Freud's *Totem and Taboo* as a myth of origins, although it's untenable in that it contains the same circle we observed concerning Levi-Strauss's explanation. According to Freud, the brothers, after the murder of their father, subsumed his law. This means it was the brothers, who were still engulfed in the order of nature, who created the condition that humanized them. That's why Lacan didn't accept it, although unlike many anthropologists he didn't fail to see its significance. Indeed, if the order of law was instituted after the murder of the father, this means that what created law was the very name of the father, since only his name remained after his death. So it was *the name* that constituted the third.

Here we approach Lacan's theory of psychosis. In the first year of his teaching Lacan introduced his famous distinctions between the symbolic father (meaning the name of the father), the imaginary father, and the real father. At the same time, he made a distinction between what he called *la parole pleine* and *la parole vide*. And with this distinction between two kinds of speech, there was a distinction between two kinds of "you." He used to ask his students, "Do you find that the *you*, the one you use in asking someone, "I don't understand what *you* said," or, "Will *you* explain this point again?" to be the same as the *you* that you use in saying to someone, "I was dazzled by the light *you* threw on this point," which is more or less a mockery? No, of course it isn't the same *you*. In the first use I was addressing myself to someone from whom I was actually expecting an answer, an Other as a place of language, while in the second mocking use, I was rather caught in the kind of aggressivity that always underlies all imaginary relations.

According to Lacan, the main characteristic of the psychotic is his incapacity to have the place of the Other in the first meaning of the word, as the place of language. For the psychotic the only other is the small other. It is true that Shreber talked about god, who was the main personage of his delirium, but for him god wasn't a third term; god was just another image of himself. For Shreber god was a cheating god, which means that god himself was taken up by the play that may go between you and me; there was no third for Shreber. You may say the possibility of thirdness was outside his mental sphere, which is the same as saying that for him the name of the father was foreclosed, the name of the father as the center of a system of names that are the names of parenthood.

You may ask, but what is there, in a system of names? "What is there in a name?" is also Juliet's question, when she remarks that a rose by any other name would smell as sweet. Here I will make a small digression to recall a remarkable, short book the title of which is *The Language Connection*, by Roy Harris. You can find it in a paperback edition (Thoemmes Press, 1996). This book constitutes a remarkable critique of the idea of metalanguage. According to Harris, the Greeks invented grammar and logic and this symbolic invention brought a real interest, that is, for a whole class of grammarians and a whole class of logicians. Defending the idea of metalanguage was a matter of assuring their livelihood. But to prove that there may be another outlook, he mentioned, among other arguments, a Chinese story about a prince who asked Confucius for counsel about what good government should be. Confucius answered, "For good government a ruler must be a ruler, a subject a subject, a father a father, and a son a son." This kind of answer tells us nothing; it seems just words, tautological. We want an answer of the sort that a ruler must be just, virtuous, and courageous, and a subject obedient, dutiful, and whatever. But our wish is nonsense, because the fact is that it is words that make the order. Words are not just the outcome of our activities; they are the regulators of our activities.

And when you think about it, no person can ensure the regularity and stability of human relations, because any person can be a cheater. Neither can it be ensured by any signification, because there is no end to significations and any signification may be put into question. So, there must be some law that is inscribed in the very name. You may say this law concerns the name of the father, as a name that is never absent in any system of names of parenthood. This doesn't mean that the father was always represented as the generator. The function of generation can be attributed to other entities, for example spirits, or ancestors, or whatever else. But the name *father* or *fathers* in the system or in the collective names of parenthood suggests the existence of the laws of marriage and signifies the prohibition of incest.

Here is an important point concerning the relation between the child and her mother. This relation, as we know, is open to all kinds of perversities. Thus, everything in this relation depends upon the degree to which the mother has herself succeeded in integrating the symbolic order, that is, the degree to which she herself has a certain respect, not so much for the person of the father as to the name of the father inasmuch as it signifies the prohibition of a perverse relation with her child. If this is the case, she may give the child all her love without being tempted to go further, to perversity. Her behavior will have far-reaching effects, because the idea of narcissism as characteristic of the child, and the idea of the *toute puissance* (omnipotence) as characteristic of the mind of the child, is false. As a matter of fact, the *toute puissance* is on the side of the mother. She gives her love, and everything. The very life of the child depends on her love. So if a child finds herself in front of this entire *toute puissance*, in front of some creature who can do anything she likes without any limit to what she can or can't do, this will have the most devastating effect. Things will take an unfortunate turn for the child if her mother behaves in such a way as to give the impression there is no limit to her caprice.

But instead of a confrontation with all this *toute puissance*, you *can* have an order of things in which the very name of the father as a third term produces its own effects, a state in which this name is substituted for her otherwise undefined desire. This substitution is the paternal metaphor, and the effect of this metaphor is to bring about some entity that does not exist in reality, in the same way that Romeo brings to light a new cosmological order when he says, "Juliet is the sun."

So what Lacan calls the paternal metaphor brings, as its effect, the creation of a new entity, which he calls the *phallic image*.[2] There is a distinction to be made here between the phallus and the penis. From this point of view the phallus isn't simply an organ of copulation; the phallus means something that can never be real. Nonetheless the possession of *it*, were it possible, would guarantee the desire of the Other, in the first place the

2. Editor's note: see pp. 59, 75.

mother's desire. And such a guarantee is simply impossible, although Othello could never understand this state of things. When he says that the curse of marriage is that it makes us believe we possess these delicate creatures when we don't possess their appetites, he reveals his blind spot. He was not content with the fact that Desdemona gave him her desire; he wanted *it* guaranteed. That's the meaning of aspiring *to be* the phallus, and the only means to *it* is to keep on going in the way of idealization. Othello speaks as if his mirror image were composed of all the perfections of the world. Of course this idealizing effort is destined to fail. There can be no other outcome because there will always be a difference between the ideal and the phallic image, which is a lack that can't be filled.

And if you go back and examine a child's relation to her mirror image once this phallic image has come into play, what will be the result? The result is that the girl will perceive a lack, and the boy will see his penis. But a boy is in no better position than a girl, since he will perceive that his penis is really pitiful, and he will have the feeling of his insufficiency, as if something were missing that would otherwise make him complete and *would* guarantee the desire of the Other.

It is at this point that we approach the heart of subjectivity. A subject is not a thing; a subject cannot have all its presence here and at once. And not being a thing, a subject is an absence. You may say with Lacan that this absence that "appears" in the mirror image is the absence where we are. This is castration as an imaginary effect of the symbolic order. The subject, however, who doesn't know where this "void" came from, will experience it as frustration. The girl will envy the boy for what he apparently possesses, and the boy will try to imagine someone else who has what he hasn't, so that he can have *it* in an indirect way, through identification with the one who has *it*, the father or father substitute, whoever it may be. But this imaginary identification will only perpetuate his frustration. The way out, which is the meaning of symbolic castration, is to stop trying to complete the mother, at any cost. The "rock of castration" is the rock of the mother's castration, which amounts to admitting that, after all, the mother is not one's own business, she's the business of the father.[3] From this point of view symbolic castration amounts to assuming a lack that, as long as it is not assumed, will leave the subject a perpetual prey to lack in the form of frustration.

Here I would like to add a point about Lacan's research, while he was giving his seminar on psychosis, when he first tried to explain the idea of foreclosure of a signifier. What does this mean? He said that if there were a signifier that didn't exist in language, it would have an incalculable effect. As a matter of fact, there is an agreeable novel by a Spanish writer, entitled *The Al-*

---

3. Editor's note: see pp. 58, 60.

phabetical Order, in which the author imagines a society where books begin to fly and words begin to disappear. The result was tremendous, because people couldn't sit anywhere, as there was no word for chair, couldn't sleep in beds, because there was no word for bed. In this way Lacan first explained foreclosure. He started with the question, "Is there in language a true signifier that doesn't figure?" And then he asked, "Where is this hole in the plane of signifiers?" He found it in the fact that there is no signifier that expresses feminine reality as such.

Let me explain this point. Obviously the words *man* and *woman* figure as subjects in an infinite number of propositions. Everyone has her own ideas about what a woman is, and each society has its own rules about the activities, the rights, and the duties of one or the other. But there is one situation in which the terms must be used not as subjects but as attributes; that is, the moment of birth. At birth you must say whether the newborn is a girl or a boy. For clear gestaltic reasons, the phallus functions as the signifier of sexual difference. This means that woman is defined not by what she is, but by what she isn't.

But does this mean that, inasmuch as a woman gets into some contact with the experience of her own femininity, she will in some measure fall victim to some psychotic position? Writers like Serge André claim that this hypothesis shouldn't be excluded, but in my opinion

Lacan didn't go that far. It's true that according to Lacan the power of the signifier in ordaining reality is eminent, and to such an extent that for him there is no direct opposition between day and night: the opposition is first between day and absence of day, and it is in the absence of day that night takes its place. But in spite of this eminence accorded to the signifier, he didn't go to the extent of explaining the foreclosure of the name of the father as an absence of the word. He had to admit to the idea of what I call a system of names of parenthood, which sustains as such the whole human order. "Father" is a word the position of which cannot be denied even to Shreber. But here it is a matter of the *use* of that signifier. From this point of view everything can go for a subject as if the word father, *insofar as it signifies a certain symbolic order*, had no existence at all. This is the angle through which one can understand the idea of the foreclosure of that signifier.

I think now you may put forth any questions that may help us go further.

Question: What does Serge André claim?

He wrote a book entitled *What Does a Woman Want?*[4] in a clear allusion to the words attributed to Freud by Ernest Jones. Freud apparently admitted to Jones that after

4. Other Press, New York, 1999.

thirty years of work he still had no answer to the question of what a woman wants. André's opinion is that women want more and more unconscious, which is why the first hysterics were so happy to have interpretations; because feminine reality is named not by what it is but by what it isn't, because there is no positive name for it, there can be only interpretations. That's the meaning of the hole or cut in the symbolic tissue. And insofar as a woman may somehow get "in touch" with this unsymbolized and un-named reality, she will find herself in this state of the fore-closure of a signifier that would say what she is. In that way she may find herself in a somehow psychotic posi-tion. This may be an exaggeration but André sees no rea-son to exclude it as a hypothesis.

He illustrates his point by using Joan Rivière's paper, "Feminine as a Masquerade." It's a clinical presentation of a patient, a woman. Although Rivière was actually delivering something about herself, she presented it as a case of a woman whose behavior was always dis-tributed two ways. First, she is brilliant, active, and splendid, which has the meaning of taking hold of the phallus. Second, she is seized by guilt, which entails the surrendering of the phallus. And this mechanism was her means of expressing her femininity, because she argues that femininity cannot be expressed except through the labyrinth of the unconscious. The woman had to create an unconscious mythology in order to sustain her masquerade status, which was better than coming face to face with her unnamed reality, a greater source of anxiety than castration itself.

Question: Lacan doesn't go that far?

I don't think that Lacan went as far as to assimilate the feminine position to the psychotic position. He was rather led to talk about feminine *jouissance* as different from phallic *jouissance*.

Question: It seems to me that grammar rules seem to disappear; there are fewer and fewer. Isn't this an example of something totally foreclosed?

If grammar disappears, there will be no language at all. Recall the sentence invented by Noam Chomsky, "Green ideas sleep furiously," as an example of a sentence that is grammatically correct but supposedly has no meaning. As a matter of fact, it does have meaning. Why not say "ideas that sleep furiously" is a metaphor for the unconscious? If you don't have the referent, you can give a sentence any meaning you like. Where there is grammar there is meaning, because you can *give* meaning to any grammatical sentence. But if there is no grammar there can be no meaning whatsoever, and then there can be no language. The idea of grammar may have been a Greek invention, but the fact remains that in every utterance there is the distribution of a subject and an attribute, in noun phrases and in verb phrases, and you will find this distribution in all languages, which is why language without grammar means the absence of language.

Question: Why can't a specific grammar be constructed or invented to prevent the possible foreclosure of the name of the father?

Since there is no language without grammar, to invent a grammar means to invent a language. But language is never invented; it is always transmitted. If it is invented, it's a failure. The example is Esperanto, which could never be a universal tongue.

Question: I understand you to be saying that when the name of the father is foreclosed you have psychosis and that the signifier for woman is absent from language, which can be seen as a form of foreclosure. Therefore, there may be a relation between femininity and psychosis. Lacan's third seminar on psychosis seems to suggest this. But you seem to be saying that Lacan pulled away from this idea.

For the moment at least I am keen to distinguish between the two cases. In one case it is a matter of the absence in language of a signifier for femininity. Femininity is always equal in the unconscious to passivity or to some other term, but it has no signifier as such. In the other case, there is a signifier, father, but it's a name whose impact never received its weight in someone's life. Everything goes for the psychotic as if this name did not exist at all. This may be the outcome or the result of her relation to her mother, inasmuch as a mother may behave as if her desire were unbridled, as not subject to any law whatsoever. But there are also cases where this devastating effect comes from the father. There are cases where the father behaves toward his son not as a model who can overcome the anxieties of the castration complex, but as someone who is himself the author of the law.

Question: You are speaking about Schreber's father?

Yes, as a matter of fact Schreber's father was something of a monster. His son remained imprisoned in a relation with some *other* person, who had nothing of the father and everything of the tyrant or elder and stronger brother. All meaning of fatherhood is bound to disappear in such a constellation.

Question: You can define evil as the absence of good, not as a positive thing. Similarly, the feminine is defined as the absence of the male. But on the other hand, the mother is this omnipotent being. So how is it that the feminine signifier is different from other words in the language? Why isn't the signifier "woman" positive?

The signifier "woman" is surely positive. The question is why there is no signifier for femininity or for sexual difference. In the *unconscious*, woman is represented negatively, as *not* marked by the signifier of the phallus. In the *unconscious* the difference between femininity and masculinity is always assimilated to the difference between passivity and activity, to what is penetrated and to what penetrates, and so on. In short there is no name in the unconscious that symbolizes the reality of the feminine. Thus woman is defined not by what she is but by what she isn't.

As to the reference to evil as the absence of good, this makes me think of theological matters in general, and in particular to what is called negative theology. We touch here an important point, which we may deal with at some other moment. I think of the object insofar as it was always considered, as an object of knowledge, as such defined or determined by its qualities and virtues. The fact, however, is that a child is loved not for her perfections but for her lack. Love enhances any trait that the object may carry and will turn it into a virtue, whatever it is. Desire is never determined by the objective qualities of the object, or by its gifts. You need only read a novel like *Portrait of a Lady* by Henry James. That's why there is nothing more antagonistic to the theology of perfection than psychoanalysis according to Lacan's conception of desire.

Question: Why do they say in Semitic languages that when a man sleeps with a woman the man gets to "know" his wife? Why isn't it said that when a woman sleeps with a man she gets to "know" her husband?

As a matter of fact, the relation to the object as an object of knowledge or of contemplation is ambiguous. It is often expressed by metaphors borrowed from the sexual field. That's why the use of mathematics from Galileo on was a big step in the direction toward getting rid of the grasp of this imagery. Why don't we say that woman knows man? Because of what I have just said, that femininity and masculinity are translated in the unconscious in terms of passivity and activity, the male being the active one. He is the knower; she is the known.

Question: When there are two human beings, regardless of gender, the active one is male?

In daily life a woman may be very active or even dominating. But this is always perceived as a masculine trait. Gender comes back.

Question: Isn't that the challenge of modern times, to define the roles for men and for women?

Social institutions vary between societies, and here there are merely points of view about what should be there, which roles should be taken by men and which by women, say in French society, or American society, or Semitic society, which is to say that the question is dealt with from the point of view of the ideal: what the ideal role is. For me the ideal role is the one that helps most in developing one's own talents.

At present there is too much talk about roles, which may be considered as a measure of the degree of embarrassment, if not anxiety, that actually characterizes the relations between the sexes. The latest law promulgated in France stipulates that every political party must present the same number of female candidates as male candidates. But trying to regulate relations between the sexes through the force of law is not only condemned to failure, it is also a declaration of fiasco.

3

Previously I spoke of the mediated character of desire, and I recalled the well known Hegelian saying, desire is the desire of the other. As a matter of fact, this mediated character was already known to Immanuel Kant. In his *Pure Practical Reason* he mentions the story of the French king who said, referring to a city his brother wanted to capture, "I want what my brother wants," from which Kant concluded that the relation between one human's will and another's cannot be anything but conflictual. In other words, you can't deduce moral law from empirical experience. I added that Lacan retained the notion of the mediated character of desire, but gave it a different turn: desire as mediated not by another ego (*le semblable*) but by the Other, with a big O, considered to be the place of language and truth. This gives desire a different character and leads to a different dialectic. And we may now remark that if desire has the capacity of bringing peace to the conflict between wills, it is because it is itself mediated by law.

Given that the Other is considered as the place of language, the question then arises, what is the elementary form of language? According to Aristotle language is there to say something; assertion is the primitive form of language. But the fact is, as Lacan remarked, the first form of speech is the demand: one first speaks not to assert something but to demand something. Now the demand is, by definition, addressed to the Other, and this experience of the Other is at the same time an experience of her desire, inasmuch as the Other will answer according to her wish, by saying either yes or no.

This experience of the Other's desire is also an experience that makes me feel that I realize in my being, at the level of worthiness or unworthiness, some intrinsic value, which is translated by the Other's acceptance or rejection of my demand. This experience of the Other's desire, inasmuch as she may answer yes or no, is moreover an experience of the commutative nature of the signifier, or of what Roman Jacobson names the metaphoric axis of language. This leads to what he calls the connective or combinatory axis, inasmuch as a child has to combine signifiers in order to articulate her demand. But what is important is that, in front of the mystery of the desire of the Other, the child is completely helpless. This experience of helplessness is the essence of what Freud calls trauma. According to Lacan it is at this very place of helplessness or anxiety that *desire is produced*, which amounts to saying that in its very essence *desire is a defense*. For Freud, as you know, all defense is defense against desire, which is fundamentally right. But according to Lacan, desire is itself defense, *a defense against the desire of the Other*.

Here one may add the precision that the subject defends herself with her ego, or with some element borrowed from the register of the imaginary relation to the Other. That's what's going on when, for example, the child transforms her shit into a gift. What this gift or offer expresses is not simply an exhibition of prestige, something akin to what takes place in the relation with a small other. What is at stake here is the subject herself; as a speaking subject she *is* the gift.

Here we grasp the originality of Lacan's theory of the fantasy. The formula of the fantasy according to him is this:

The barred S is the subject herself, the speaking subject as such, marked by the effects of the signifier. The letter *a* is the element borrowed from the imaginary field. The function of the fantasy is to fix and define the subject's desire, which is why human desire has the property of being coordinated not to real objects, but to fantasies. This conception of desire entails an answer to the question of what the unconscious means: it means that the subject never enjoys complete possession of her being, that there is always some distance between her and this being of her, which forbids attaining *it* except, as Lacan says, through that metonymy of being called desire. For example, she attains *it* in the aforementioned anal object.

What is the reason for this so-called flight of being? It is clear that being would not escape us if there could be a complete and definite answer to the question, what am I? In other words, being escapes the subject because, at the level in which the subject is engaged in its relation to the Other as the place of language and truth, there is no signifier that can answer this question. According to Lacan, however, this lack of a signifier is itself a signifier, and is indicated in the unconscious by a signifier, namely the phallus. But in his seminar on desire and its interpretation, Lacan said that the lacking signifier is the phallus, which seems to be a contradiction, since the very fact of naming *it* seems to be proof that it doesn't lack. Before giving this answer, however, and for no other apparent reason than to relax his audience, he gave a narration of a witticism, which Darwin had mentioned in his book about the expression of emotions, because it somehow started him off.

The story was that Darwin had attended a meeting in British high society where people were socializing, when they began to discuss Lady York, who was very old and gravely ill. I mean everybody there knew her days were numbered. Then an Englishman said something to the effect, "I heard Lady York was overlooked," and everyone immediately understood that she was overlooked by death. Thus, the man succeeded in evoking death without calling it by name. And that's what caught Darwin's attention, how you can say something without naming it.

The moral of the story is that you can't say what death *is*, even if you do name it, because in this sense a name is insufficient. Suppose the man had said, "I hear Lady York hasn't yet died," this would not presentify death, it would simply be news. Or suppose he even went so far as to say, "I wish Lady York would die"; this would simply be a death wish. And, as a matter of fact, a death wish completely masks death as "the final destiny" or as "the final word of life," or as "the last judgment," or as "the absolute master." Even here you see I can't name it, I can only accumulate metaphors. Of course we can talk about death inasmuch as it structures life. We can say, for example, that it is because we forget death at almost every moment of our lives that at the end of our lives we feel as though we were strangers to all we had lived, to all we had gone through. But to talk about it as a structure is not the same as saying what death *is*.

The same thing is true for the phallus, inasmuch as it is *articulated only in the unconscious*. I mean that speaking about the way it structures our relation to language, or to the Other as the place of language, or to the unconscious, is different than saying what it is. Like death, the phallus lies outside the field of representation; we can only "represent" it through metaphor. This means that we cannot, so to speak, put our hand on it, and if we do it's something else, for example the fetish.

There is a point here that must be underlined. I said two things: (1) there is no signifier that can tell us what we are, and (2) this signifier is the phallus. Suppose I had stopped with the first assertion. This would mean all talk is in vain, because nothing definite could ever be said, and that what is between you and me is simply absence of any definition, that is, absence of any true answer. And then you would have to say that speech is a complete stranger to the dimension of truth, which would not be able to find its place in this state of things. But Freud's experience shows there is a point to speaking, and that point is castration. A fear of passivity in the man; this for him was the rock that couldn't be crossed.[1] (Whether it is as rocky as all that and whether there may be a means to traverse it is another question.) What is important is that there is a point to speech, and the point takes its shape as castration, independent of

1. Editor's note: see pp. 42, 56, 60, 68.

the question of whether or not it can be surmounted or overcome. And it is precisely because lack proves itself at the end of the psychoanalytic experience as having a definite point (the point called phallic) that the dimension of truth comes into play, as introduced in discourse.

It is interesting here to notice that it is the lack in the set of signifiers that brings about the lack in the imaginary, mentioned earlier when I said that the paternal metaphor engenders an imaginary object. In fact, it is an object that can never appear, not even in the imaginary. It's a case of something imaginary that isn't specular, a case of *that* which escapes the image. It is more like a thought of an image than an image. It *appears* in the mirror *as an absence*,[2] regarding which the boy feels his insufficiency and the girl her lack. That's why the girl sees her image through the image of the other sex, where her lack seems to be defined, and that's why the boy seeks the cancellation of his insufficiency in the image of his father or father substitute, the image of the leader he supposes is not insufficient. In each case the mirror image is marked by a break or cut from *that*, which would have made each of them complete and perfect. This is the precise cut or lack that mediates all object relations, in the case of the girl or the boy, since otherwise each of them would be drowned in complete sufficiency, in complete narcissistic satisfaction with her

2. Editor's note: see pp. 40, 75.

or his own image. That's why we may say there is nothing like primary narcissism in the sense of a complete one. Primary narcissism is rather an inspiration.

To repeat: this imageless image of the phallic object appears only as absence and this absence is the very absence where we are. At this place where being lacks, the lack through the operation of the paternal metaphor proves to be the lack of being the phallus, or of castration. The subject tries to cancel this lack by imagining that the Other possesses the object she lacks, so that she may recuperate her completeness through identification with that Other. This is the mechanism of idealization, which usually goes with the movement of what Freud calls regression from object relations to identifications. Idealization inaugurates identification with the object.

This means that accession to object relations proper goes hand in hand with the perception of the lack of being, or of being the phallus as a lack, which is as well shared by the Other as by the subject herself. The rock of castration is, in the final account, the rock of castration of the Other.[3] Here we touch the point of the desire of the analyst.

But for the moment, let us return to the question of the interpretation of desire. To deal with this question we have to add some words concerning desire in

3. Editor's note: see p. 42.

its relation to the demand. Lacan's first reflections concerning this difference between desire and demand probably began with his reading of Freud's Jewish stories. Most of them are stories of demands made by people of humble means. What brings about the comic character of these stories and the pleasure we take in them comes from the revelation of the desires that the demands disguise. That's why a simple answer to the demand misses the point, the point of desire. The demand is for a small sum of money, but the desire is to eat salmon mayonnaise. The demand is to be cured from an ailment, but the desire is to enjoy the most expensive spa in the world. The subject not only borrows from the Other her signifiers as the place of language, *she borrows only those signifiers the Other authorizes her to take*. The articulation of the demand is submitted to a certain censorship.

Another point regarding the distinction between desire and demand concerns the evolution of the relation between the mother and her child. Lacan distinguishes between two moments. In the first moment the mother has value only as a presence or as an absence, that is, she is symbolic; she has no value other than that she is either here or not here, and the object itself is an object that is real, which brings out its effects concerning the satisfaction of needs without the child being aware of it. You may say that while the mother is symbolic, the object is real.

The second phase begins when the child starts making demands for herself. When the child becomes the agent of the demand, the first state of things is reversed. Then the mother becomes real, in the sense that she becomes a power that can either give or refuse to give, while the object becomes symbolic, as a mere sign of love. Then the demand, if I may say so, becomes double. It is an expression of need, but at the same time it's a demand for love, or for a sign of love. This means that the object, since it's been reduced simply to its value as a sign of love and nothing more, loses its particularity. If an object fails to function as a sign of love, the child won't give a damn for it. The exact wording of the demand at this level is not, "Give me *this* object," but "Give me this object to *show me you love me.*"

But then, curiously enough, our experience shows that the object reappears as an object of desire, that is, as an absolute condition without which there is no possible satisfaction. It is inasmuch as the breast, for example, is neither an object of need nor an object of love that it functions as the cause of oral desire. This means that it is in the interval, between the demand as an expression of need and the demand as an expression of love, that the object regains its particularity as an object of desire, which as such can be described by a double negation: it is neither a sign of love nor an object of need. What is the reason for this return of particularity?

Here we join up with what was already said about desire being defense. *The return of particularity is the very condition for there being a subject at all.* Indeed, it is through the production of desire as an absolute condition that the subject is not simply a living puppet, at the disposal of the Other, although she may come to identify herself with the object of the Other's desire, through confusing the Other's desire with the Other's demand. This enables us to understand why the subject is so keen to defend her desire as such, *by keeping it away from satisfaction*, and so much so that you may say the subject doesn't even want what she desires. Recall the dream of the butcher's beautiful wife. Although she desired caviar, she didn't want it, which is why we may say that her desire was the Other's desire. To Freud, all defense is defense against desire, and we now see what this means: all defense is defense against the satisfaction of desire.[4] Or, you may say again, *all defense is defense against the lack of the lack.*

The experience that first attracted Lacan's attention to this paradoxical status of the object of desire seems to have been the phenomenon relating to feminine sexuality.[5] At some moment in her development a little girl demands the phallus from her mother, a

4. Editor's note: see pp. 55, 77.
5. Editor's note: see pp. 46, 72, 78.

demand as alienated from the natural order of things as anything can be. It amounts to demanding the impossible. A little girl asks her mother, "Mother, give me *something*," with it being completely understood that nothing the mother can give will ever be that *something*. One may say that things go this way because such an impossible demand is what maintains her as a subject of the signifier (she can always go on demanding) and therefore as a subject of language. So here we are able to see, in its full ambiguity, the state of desire. It is structured like a demand, but it goes in the opposite direction. Its objects (for example, caviar for the butcher's beautiful wife) are only metonymic signifiers of unsatisfied desire. (But this is not a catastrophe; it simply means that the only satisfaction that can be given to a desire is not the attainment of an object, but the gift of a complementary lack.)

Since one may say, however, that the subject both desires and doesn't desire the metonymic object, how then is interpretation possible? To answer this question, Lacan mentions a dream that was reported by Freud in his paper, "Formulations on the Two Principles of Mental Functioning,"[6] where he speaks about the pleasure principle and the reality principle. At the end of this short paper he reports the dream of a man whose father had

6. *Standard Edition* 12:213–226.

died after a long illness that had caused his father terrible suffering. Right after his father's death, this man dreamed he was standing in front of his father and his father was talking to him and in this dream he felt immense pain because he realized that his father was dead but didn't know it. Freud says this absurd dream becomes completely intelligible when you add to the phrase "that he was dead," "according to the dreamer's wish."[7] This implies that for Freud interpreting this dream consisted in restoring the omitted part of the phrase to the analysand.

But may we consider this to be the kind of interpretation that ought to be given to an analysand? His dream is a fantasy, which has an element that comes from the imaginary: his father appears, as the object of his rivalry, and it is from this rivalry that the subject may forget the possibility of his own death. So we may indeed suppose that his father's death struck him so closely he had to regress to his old oedipal wish, in order to restore the figure of his father as his rival. But if that's so, what's the point of restoring the omitted part of the phrase to him? While it's true it was omitted, this very omission is itself a signifier, a signifier of his refusal to equalize his own destiny to that of his father's, which is why he regressed to the *primal* father image. So, the

7. *Standard Edition* 5:430–431.

question is then: If the dream's wish lies in this fantasy, what about the analysand's desire outside his dream? Is his desire outside his dream to be awakened to what we may call the dream's message as betrayed by the omission in the text of the dream, or is it to not be awakened to this message, and to keep on refusing his mortal reality?

It is true that the subject's desire outside the dream was also a fantasy, which is why one may say that his waking life was something of a dream. But a fantasy is a lie, and as such it is the negation of some truth. And by coming to light it indicates the presence of that truth. So the question may be put again: Is the analysand's desire to be told his fantasy, or is it to be enabled to recognize the message of his dream?

This example shows that the difference between the dream wish and desire corresponds fairly to the two mediations we began by recalling. We saw the Hegelian view of mediation, that the desire of the small other leads to rivalry and generates a lack, which is frustration. But according to Lacan, the symbolic order introduces a different form of lack, which is called castration. And you may say, using this example of the dream related by Freud, that desire consists precisely in interpretation, if we mean by this word *the acknowledgment of the dream's message*.

Question: Could you say more on the gift of a complementary lack?

Suppose you go out with a friend, and she sees a particular object that she likes, perhaps a vase or a lamp. This may be considered as an expression of her desire, but it doesn't imply that she necessarily wants to acquire that object. To give her the object is not for sure the way to answer her desire. But suppose you happen to have the same appreciation for that particular object and you express it at the same time, this coincidence between two desires will surely be a source of joy for both of you. Similarly, if a girl falls in love, what she wants in exchange, if one may say so, is not any particular object; she will find certain satisfaction in no other gift than that of your own love, your lack. This is a point that is at the source of many misunderstandings, because we normally consider a gift to be of something we have, not of something we haven't.

Question: What are the consequences for psychoanalysis when you have a lacking subject who comes to analysis thinking that the analyst is complete and has the answer to his lack? Do you say that the best gift is to show him that you are lacking too?

The analyst doesn't proceed like Socrates in *The Symposium*. Of course Alcibiades's transference consisted in his idealization of Socrates. He makes recourse to the simile of the *agalma*, of the little boxes with ugly figures on the outside, but hidden inside is a beautiful statue of

divine being. So Socrates was for Alcibiades the
iner of the unknown, the thing that is good. What
ιat is good he doesn't say, but he says that Socrates
 container of *it*. In this you see an example of the
 as idealized, as containing what I must have, at
rice. Specifically, Alcibiades was a man of power-
·sire; he was passionate. But Socrates could see that
iades's declaration was an act of deception, deceiv-
mself and the Other by the same token. So, Socrates'
:r consisted of telling him he was mistaken, because
In't have any of the gold Alcibiades had put into him.
The analyst doesn't proceed by making a declara-
o the effect that she is nothing, or that the patient
:eiving her. Being nothing is an existential fact. It
d be proved through *acts*. It is usually sufficient for
ιalyst to abstain from subscribing to the analysand's
sies, although she may question those fantasies. For
ple, in the dream concerning the dead father, there
n absurdity. The dream said that the father was dead
ut knowing it. The analyst may make the remark
after all, one can't be both dead and know it. That's
an analyst should proceed, among other ways, as
ician. Freud signaled it; we all remember his re-
s on absurdity in dreams, and similar topics. Be-
 avoiding imprisoning him in his fantasy, such an
·ould bring, if not a liberation, at least a revision
 fantasy, and by the same token it would signify
he analyst's desire is not situated on the same level

as the analysands, inasmuch as the latter is engulfed in rivalry. So you see that it all goes through the analyst's desire.

Question: What are some of the other ways an analyst should proceed?

The other ways are many. You may proceed as a rhetorician, or as a dialectician, not to mention situations where you must put a limit to a certain behavior, or sometimes you may need to confirm the truth of what has just been said. It is always a matter of what is suitable in the moment. In psychoanalysis, readiness is all.

Question: If idealization is the first step in the process of identification, could you speak about where identification goes beyond idealization; how does it move beyond that?

There is a well known chapter in Freud's book *Group Psychology and the Analysis of the Ego*,[8] entitled "Identification." In this short chapter he names three kinds of identification. The third one is hysterical identification, which he describes as identification with another's desire. The example is identification with another girl, without any idealization.

8. *Standard Edition* 18:107.

Question: You contrasted imaginary frustration with symbolic castration. What is the relation of this to privation?

When you say the book is not on the shelf, what is not at its place, as Lacan aptly remarks, is not the real object or the real book. The real is always where it is. The lack here is attributed to the book only inasmuch as it exists in language, that is, in the symbolic. You may say, using Jeremy Bentham's vocabulary, the lack is attributed to the book inasmuch as it is a *fictive entity*, a term by which Bentham meant things that only exist in language, such as "right," "wrong," "property," and "law," or at least could never exist without language, like the very idea of place such as "north," "west," and so on. But the lack itself, insofar as you can see the hole on the shelf, is real. So here, the object is symbolic, but the lack is real. The main example of privation concerns the woman's lack of a penis. You can't say that she lacks a real organ, any more than she lacks a third eye. The object here is symbolic, a woman actually has more sexual organs than a man, but what is real is the lack.

With frustration, the lack is imaginary and the object is real. This is why nothing can satisfy frustration, because frustration is not a real lack. The main example here is the so-called penis envy, where the object envied is indeed a real organ, but it is clear that the lack itself is imaginary: She can't feel this lack without imagining it.

In castration, the object, that is, the phallus, is an imaginary object, but here it a question of an image that escapes the specular order. It may be considered rather as a hole than as part of this order. As to the lack itself, it is clearly symbolic, inasmuch as it is in the nature of an act of recognition. This means recognition that the phallus, taken as a signifier of the mother's lack, points here to a lack that should be directed to the father and that he should answer.

In short, in privation the lack is real and the object is symbolic, while in frustration the lack is imaginary and the object is real. And in castration the lack is symbolic and the object is imaginary. But in each case there is discordance between the register of lack and that of the object.

Question: Could you review again something about the subject, the subject is not a thing but an absence? It sounds like you are giving the subject agency to do things, to identify and so on. How can the subject be both absence and agency?

The distinction between the ego and the subject amounts to a distinction between what is transparent and what is not, and it is in that sense absent. But it is precisely because of this lack that the subject becomes an agent, for example, by proceeding to identify. It is out of her lack that she is an agent.

Question: Do you think there is a biological basis for the unconscious?

No. Everything I have said can only be taken as proof of how far the unconscious is from having a biological basis, of the subversion of the biological by the signifier. Take the example of the girl who asks her mother to give her the phallus. ("Mother, give me 'something'"!) This can in no case be explained as in harmony with any biological or natural order, such as is the case with needs, where the lack is real, say hunger, and the object is also real, say food. That's why I have just underlined the discordance between the lack and the object for human subjects. This discordance is the proof par excellence that we are dealing with an order of conflicts that has no solution in the plans of nature. There is no biological reason why the oral instinct manifests itself in man as a cannibalistic drive. Whenever you try to understand the psychoanalytic state of things, with desire or with the demand for love, you will only witness the subversion of all natural relations, which succumb to something else as a result of our relation to the signifier, as a result of our state as speaking subjects, taken in by language.

Question: In the Freudian theory of the drives, the passive and active aims of the drives, isn't there anything at all on the side of nature?

There may be passive and active attitudes observable in the relations among animals, but these attitudes don't function as metaphors for masculinity and femininity. That's what makes the difference, their utilization as signifiers, for signification.

Question: Is the progress of analysis from privation through frustration to castration? Is analysis this progression?

No. You may describe psychoanalysis as a mediation that enables the subject to overcome her frustration, not by joining the object of her desire or by acceding to some kind of mythical organic completeness, but by assuming another register of lack, which we characterized as symbolic castration. In the dream of the dead father, dead without knowing he was dead, if the analysand remains caught up in his position of rivalry with his father as the means to avoid acknowledging his own mortality, this would amount to remaining in a state of perpetual frustration. That's why an interpretation that tells him his fantasy of rivalry, if it brings him any news at all, will do nothing, if I may say so, to serve him. The point is not to tell the fantasy but to discover its function; in this example it functions as a denial of death, of castration.

4

We have alluded more than once to the operation called the paternal metaphor, which, needless to say, takes place behind the subject's back, as the subject only suffers its effects. The effects are double: on the one hand she represents the phallus for her mother, and on the other, since she merely represents it, she isn't the phallus. Thus she is at the same moment both crowned her majesty the baby, and demoted. You may ask, wherein lies this symbolic castration?

In fact, the subject is demoted by symbolic castration from the very beginning, a demotion that assigns her the task of assuming a particular kind of lack, which manifests itself on the imaginary level as an insufficiency that marks her mirror image. At the same time desire has only two faces; with one face it is the law and with the other it is transgression. Here you may say that the subject lies in this lack itself,[1] she *is* this lack, the phallus, which Lacan symbolizes by -φ.

1. Editor's note: see pp. 40, 59, 71.

The phallus (or -φ) is an unconscious signifier, but the fact of naming it won't capture its workings as an unconscious signifier. In fact even the pregenital objects function in our experience as phallic objects, which is why we talk of the phallic breast and the phallic feces. Here we may measure how far we are from any biological conception of the object, or in other words how far we are from the conception, according to which development consists in the integration of the so-called partial objects, which are destined to be synthesized into what's called the formation of the total object, that is, the genital object. This latter conception is plainly contrary to what Freud frequently repeats, that desire finds its satisfaction in the field of hallucination, which amounts to saying that desire goes against the construction of reality.

Lacan approached the question of the object of desire, named the *obj. a*, from several points of view. We may begin with the remark that language contains what is called a shifter, that is, a first-person pronoun, which denotes the speaker. In English it's the pronoun *I*. There is always, however, something that escapes this denotation, which is precisely the thing that I am as the author or agent of the denotation. In other words, when the subject *appears* in the phrase as the subject of the enunciated, she *disappears* as subject of the enunciation. This distinction between the two was introduced by Jacobson, although Lacan gives it a much more far-reaching significance than it's given by grammarians. Disappearance as the subject of the enunciation whenever she appears in the pronoun *I* is what Lacan calls the fading or *aphanisis* of the subject, a word he took from Jones, although Jones used it to describe a kind of dread he conceived as being a dread of the disappearance of desire.

This "disappearance" of the subject, however, is not a simple return to nothingness. It rather means that the subject is in lack of herself. We may allude here to the common expression, "I don't even know myself." And here comes the *obj. a,* inasmuch as it gives some form to this lack, which nonetheless doesn't mean that the *obj. a* is an object one wants to get or to have. It's rather what Freud calls an essentially lost object and the subject is more likely to experience anxiety over the prospect of having this object, that is, anxiety over losing this loss, or of lacking this lack, because this would amount to her disappearance as desire, which is, according to Spinoza, the essence of man. In other words, the *obj. a* is rather the cause of desire, that is, the cause and the signifier of desire, that is, it functions from behind, and not as an object, so to speak, "in front," such as any common object, even though we may search for it in the field of common objects.

In other words we may say that the *obj. a* is the subject's lost name, her name as the subject of the enunciation. That's why Lacan goes so far as to say that whenever there is an *I* in a statement, there is the *obj. a* on the level of enunciation. It is the name of the subject of the enunciation, as articulated in the unconscious, and as could never be articulated in the conscious.

For example, take the oral object, which is an object the subject first considered to be part of her own body, but from which she's been mutilated or severed, and which may thus subsist as such, as the cause of her desire beyond all that is expressed in her articulated demands. And the same thing applies to the anal object. Lacan doesn't deny the notion of stages or phases but he considers these phases not as moments in biological maturation, but as corresponding to the level of apprehension the subject has of the Other. On the oral level the mother, insofar as she is the first to take the place of the Other, is the person to whom the demand is addressed. In the anal phase, the demand emanates from the Other and is addressed to the subject who, so to speak, answers, by giving part of herself.

These two phases concern detachable objects. But if we go to the third one, the so-called phallic phase, which is where the child becomes aware of her mother's desire as such, as sexual desire, we notice that there is no lack of the phallus, at least not concerning the boy, who is by definition, if one may say so, phallophore. But this is precisely the level at which the law comes into play, because there can be no desire, once again as the essence of man, except insofar as there is lack. *This applies to sexual desire*. And that's why the name of the father must intervene here in such a way as to produce that particular form of lack, which we have specified as symbolic castration.

One of the main points in Lacan's seminar, *The Ethics of Psychoanalysis*, is the distinction between "wish" in the sense of a pious wish (it brings nothing, it's not meant to be realized) and "desire." A wish is a fantasy and a fantasy is a lie, in that in fantasy I am what I am not or I am not what I am. For example, I am not Hirsch-Hyacinth, a poor lottery vendor and pedicurist, I'm really Salomon Rothschild, the richest man in the world. I allude here to the famous story told by Heinrich Heine, about some poor fellow called Hirsch-Hyacinth (the double *H* is probably an indication of some self-irony) that Freud cites in his book, *Jokes and Their Relation to the Unconscious*.[2] Hirsch-Hyacinth was talking about the great familiarity with which his excellency Salomon Rothschild had received him. But when he was about to say "familiarity," he accidentally said, "famillionarity." The lapsus brought his lie to light, and this coming to light amounted to an involuntary confrontation with truth. You may say the truth was the message of the lapsus, which we receive by laughing.

2. *Standard Edition* 8.

The same thing applies to the dream of the father who was dead without knowing it. In this dream Freud only noticed the oedipal fantasy of rivalry with the father, which according to him constituted the latent content of the dream. But the coming to the fore of this rivalry a very short time after his father's death was to all appearances a regression, meaning a mechanism of defense. And in this conjunction, the defense was against what may be perceived, through his father's death, as their common destiny. So, there is something more here than just the oedipal fantasy, something Lacan calls the "message of the dream." And this is why interpretation is a delicate matter. To tell the subject his fantasy is really a *hopeless* operation. But neither can you tell him that his dream was a regression, a defense, or a flight from death. If you do that, you are treating his fear of death as if it were like running a red light; why not write him a ticket? As a matter of fact, during the period of his father's painful illness, the analysand had consciously had this wish. His father had suffered so greatly that he had really wished for his father to die, to deliver his father from pain. Lacan suggested that one way to approach the sharp edge of this dream, meaning its message, would be to remind the analysand of the wish he'd once expressed, adding of course that it had been for the relief of his father. I mean you may acknowledge such a wish, as it was felt by the analysand himself during his father's suffering, and this would at least be a first approach to what was at stake.

The difference between the wish and the message implied by the coming to light of the fantasy, in the signification of the fantasy, is precisely what the subject is meant to cross, according to Freud's dictum, "*Wo es war, soll Ich werden.*" And it is this *distance*, between the point where the subject *is* in his fantasy and the *truth*, that makes us talk about what is called the *l'heure de la vérité* (hour of truth); that's the hour at which the subject assumes her true condition as lack. The whole business of psychoanalysis may be considered as a realization of Freud's dictum.

Here we touch what Lacan says in his seminar *The Ethics of Psychoanalysis*, namely that where the subject gives up her desire we can be sure there is some guilt. Jones says, in his description of the boy's Oedipus complex, that when a boy finds himself in a situation where he must choose between the object and the phallus, he will choose the object, that is, the mother, and renounce the phallus. But contrary to Jones, Lacan affirms that the subject chooses to keep going in the way to be the phallus, in other words, that he chooses the phallus and he lets the object go, the way a hunter may prefer his rifle to his prey. Here lies the significance of giving up desire and here you may be sure there is guilt. The general opinion, that guilt is linked to getting the object, is belied by a fact anyone can notice, which is that letting go of the object doesn't bring any relief from guilt. According to Lacan, it's precisely this turning away from the object that is, if not the guilt itself, the sign of guilt.

It is in this same seminar that Lacan introduces the notion of *la Chose*, as an equivalent to the German *das Ding*, that is, the Thing. From this one may define the Thing as being the point where the Other's word (in the sense of speech but also in the sense of "giving one's word") has no guarantee. What guarantees one word is just another one, there is no way of going out of it, no way of getting out of language, and in this sense there is no metalanguage. Consequently the Thing is the very point where the Other's desire is revealed, as a complete mystery. That's the point we already referred to as the point of trauma, the point in front of which the subject feels completely helpless. According to Lacan the Freudian notion of *Hilflosigkeit* has no other meaning than helplessness in front of the enigma of the Other's desire, the mother's in the first place. One may consequently say that the Thing is beyond all representation, a fact Lacan expresses by saying that on the level of representation the Thing is *no-thing*. However, it is from this point of *das Ding*, the Thing, that the whole motion of representations is initiated. It is from the Thing that is, so to speak, behind us, that the movement of representations is launched in which the subject pursues her good according to the pleasure principle. And we have already seen that it is also at this point that the paternal metaphor replaces the enigma of the Other's (the mother's in the first place) lack, by a lack that, if it can't be said, can be signified as castration.

It is worth noting that castration, as considered here, is the effect of the name of the father, inasmuch as it works as a name through which an order of law is substituted for what would have otherwise been an order, if one may call it that, of unbridled desire. This means that castration must first be considered an effect of the signifier. The function of the real father comes later on, although this doesn't imply any diminution of its importance. According to Freud, the father function was simply natural. But Lacan considered the function to be fundamentally normative; the father's role is to support or, so to speak, give voice to prohibitions that alone may enable the subject to find her way to the realm of desire.

Here we see more clearly the difference between Levi-Strauss and Lacan concerning the question of the prohibition of incest. We have already seen that, according to Levi-Strauss, exchange is the reason for the prohibition of incest. According to him, given the dyadic structure of human relations that makes it impossible to ensure pacification between the *semblebles* or between the egos, society can't be viable without proceeding to exchange. Herein lies the necessity of the laws of marriage, that is, of the exchange of women among the human groups, of which the prohibition of the mother is only one aspect according to Levi-Strauss. In fact, this conception doesn't explain incest par excellence, incest between mother and son. And indeed, why not suppose that a mother could initiate her son into sexual life? This is a common enough obsessional fantasy, and why couldn't one of her functions be to initiate him before he enters into marriage? There is absolutely nothing in Levi-Strauss's theory that prohibits such incest.

According to Lacan, however, the demands are first addressed to the mother, and the mother is the one who gives all the objects of the demand. In Kleinian terms she is the "universal container," and in this sense she is the Supreme Good. Enjoying her would mean the end of the entire world of the demand. Thus the prohibition of the mother–son incest[3] is precisely the condition without which there can be no subsistence for the subject as a subject of demand, that is, as a subject of the signifier. You *must* have something more to demand. In brief, as Lacan says, the Supreme Good does not exist because the Supreme Good (that's the mother) is prohibited. And, according to Lacan, here lies the foundation of moral law, as reversed by Freud. Lacan goes so far as to say that all the talk about beyond good and evil is only a way of dodging the real issue. You

3. Editor's note: see p. 38.

can't go beyond evil; you can only fall into it. There is only going beyond good.

It was in his next seminar on *Transference* that Lacan put into the forefront his thesis that the desire of the analyst constitutes the axis of analysis. We have already seen how the notion of countertransference merely served as an alibi for analysts' failures. This led some analysts like Macalpine to consider transference as an artifact of the analytic situation itself, and as such akin to suggestion and subjugation. Lacan is far from such a point of view. His view is that psychoanalysis puts into question, and more seriously than ever before, what is called authentic love (*Eine echte Liebe*). To Lacan transference is the proof of the narcissistic character of all love. But besides this consideration, Lacan had another reason for his conception that the desire of the analyst is the axis at the center of analysis or of the psychoanalytic experience. Indeed, one of the axioms of his doctrine, if one may call it that, is that desire *is* the desire of the analyst. For Lacan the analyst is not the Other but is one who occupies the place of the Other, and from this it follows that the very presence of the analysand in the psychoanalytic situation amounts to a question relating to the analyst's desire, since it is only through this question addressed to the Other, or to the one who occupies the place of the Other, that the subject can have access to her own desire.

In fact, the analyst knows that there is no object that can afford the answer to this question. In other words, desire can't be said to be a desire of this or of that. But desire may be signified, and it is signified, as a lack, so the only thing the analyst can give to such a question is her silence. That is, she limits her own desire to the function of preserving the void wherein resounds the question, *Che vuoi?* What do you want me to be? Thus having no answer that offers an object to her question (an object that would be, as one may say, only a hallucination of the cause), the analysand will have to bring in the signifiers of her own desire, as reconstructed in her relations with those who first occupied the place of the Other for her, mainly the parents. So, why does transference love come into this process?

Here I would like to make the preliminary remark that transference doesn't necessarily mean the analysand falls openly in love with her analyst. It may as often be the case that there is a repressed love, that is, a love that resists avowal: it may be signified in the return of the repressed, but never said. And an analyst must have an unbelievable measure of narcissism to claim it, that is, to say she is the beloved of her patient, so if she does say it, she most often presents it as if it were a repetition. Moreover, once in the psychoanalytic situation, the analysand may rescue her narcissism by falling in love with some other object, a phenomenon called "lateral transference." But we miss the point if we don't see that lateral transference is transference.

To return to the thesis advanced in his seminar on transference, since Lacan was not yet in possession of his theory of *the subject supposed to know* as the foundation of transference, the answer he gave is that to love somebody is the best way to mislead her or to deceive her about her own lack. One may say that the natural place of a human being is in being loved, and one way to be sure you're in this place of being loved is to fall in love yourself, because by falling in love, one at least ensures one's right to be loved, or one's rights to the place of the beloved. That's why Lacan says love is a metaphor, meaning that it is an operation through which the beloved becomes the lover, wherein lies the miracle of love as exemplified by Achilles for Patrocles and by the example of Alcestis, because it is in the nature of giving love to imply the affirmation of being loved. The affirmation is intrinsic even when it isn't real; that's why Lacan says love is always reciprocal. Other analysts have said that all love is a demand for love, which again amounts to an affirmation of the narcissistic nature of this phenomenon.

However, love, being a lack rather than filling lack, brings out the question of the cause of the lack. That's the question of what *is* the object that the Other contains, which I don't know and which is that for which I love her or for which she is loved. And here comes the object of desire as described before, that is, as an intrinsically or essentially lost object, which the Other possesses no more than the subject herself, love being the means to mislead the Other concerning this lack, through a "making believe" that she contains it. So there's no wonder Lacan spotted the *obj. a* in that mysterious object described as the *agalma*, of which Alcibiades was so proud to have been the only one to glimpse in the idealized or incomparable Socrates.

It should again be noted that, considered in itself and not in its disguise, the *obj. a* is a part of one's own body, from which the subject was severed or mutilated, and which thus functions as a lack *and* as a pointer of lack. Considered from this angle, one may say it is the root of identity and, as we have already said, the lost name of the subject of enunciation. But we can now also see how much it would be the root of the uncanny were it ever to appear in the field of perception. Here is the very basis of anxiety, as exemplified by Freud's article on the uncanny,[4] where the hero was under the obligation of completing the puppet with his own eyes, and where eyes were presented as objects for collection, or even for marketing. That's why Lacan says in his seminar on anxiety that the *obj. a* is an object whose sole subjective structure is this effect.

4. *Standard Edition* 17:217–252.

Question: What about the *obj. a* as "the nothing"?

Nothing amounts to the refusal of the object in order to hold onto castration. That's why you can say in anorexia, the subject eats nothing, nothing here being the very form of oral desire, nothing being the first oral object. The nothing is the guardian of desire, it means refusing the object in order to keep one's desire.

Question: Why is desire ethical?

According to the received theory, libidinal development or maturation is linear. It goes from the oral phase through the anal phase to the phallic, or more precisely to the phallo-narcissistic phase. Here the boy at least is confronted with the threat of castration, the agent of which is the imaginary father. And it is under the pressure of this threat that the boy renounces his mother and accedes or gets access to the so-called genital object. But according to Lacan, castration, as an effect of substitution, is already there; the gap (*beance*) of castration is at the very center. And it is inasmuch as this gap is assumed by the subject, whether a girl or a boy, that she or he receives access to a desire in conformance with her or his sex. And, it is only inasmuch as the subject refuses this gap, that is, inasmuch as she refuses castration as a symbolic debt, that she regresses to the anal phase, or to the oral phase, and that's why these objects always function in our experience as phallic objects. Once again we talk about the phallic feces or the phallic breast. It is this very fact of desire being a function of law, not to say that it *is* law, that gives desire its ethical status. Inasmuch as she refuses the lack, she can't escape castration as a debt. Once again, all this is implied in Freud's dictum, mentioned in our preceding developments.

Question: I didn't really grasp the question of *das Ding*. Lacan refers to the counterpart divided into two parts and the relation of *das Ding* to the counterpart?

If by counterpart you mean what Freud called *Nebenmensch*, the idea has a simple meaning. There is some person who accomplished what Freud calls the specific actions for the child. The child is helpless, and unable to effectuate or accomplish certain necessary actions so that she can gain the objects of her needs, for example food. So someone does it for her. The person who performs the actions may be, so to speak, divided into two parts; one part that is liable to change, such as with gestures and facial expressions, and another part that remains the same, such as the face in itself, a "part" that Freud calls the *nucleus*, which is recognized without being understood. A gesture may convey a meaning, but a face is either recognized or it's not.

But Lacan gave this notion a widely different meaning. He took it to mean that in my relation to the *Nebenmensch* or to put it in French, the *prochain*, that is, my neighbor, as in "love thy neighbor as thyself," *the Other*, there's some part that can never be assimilated, that cannot be articulated, that cannot be brought into transparency, that is, the point of the Other's desire as enigma.[5] That's the point of the Thing. Lacan gives an example of someone very dear to you putting you in an embarrassing situation. You are so embarrassed you have no other recourse than to utter the word, "You!" He describes it as a you of incantation, of name taming, by which I mean a taming that tames nothing. Lacan says this you is *le mot de la Chose*, a phrase that can have no translation in English, because the word *mot* in the French language is opposed to *parole*, an opposition that doesn't exist in English.

Question: At the supreme moment of love, the only way to answer is by saying *You*?

No, at the supreme moment of *embarrassment*. There are some moments of embarrassment in front of the Other, the Other being man for a woman and woman for a man, when you have no other recourse except "*Tu*," in the two meanings of the word in French, that is, as second-person pronoun, and as kept in silence.

5. Editor's note: see pp. 54, 82.

Addendum

Question: As this is our last meeting, Mr. Safouan, is there a moment for you to say something about the practice of psychoanalysis? For example, why don't you need to wait until completing analysis to begin practicing analysis?

The regulations of the International Psychoanalytic Association stipulate that a candidate must first finish her didactic analysis, and only afterward, if she is authorized to do so, may she begin to practice psychoanalysis. But it's common knowledge that candidates don't generally wait until this end. For one thing, a candidate always has the possibility of beginning to take patients into analysis without calling what she does "analysis." For example, she may see a patient three times a week, and then pretend it isn't really analysis, because analysis should be a minimum of four times a week. So, as always happens when there is a rule, you witness the ways the rule can be circumvented. In the Lacanian circles, we just took note of this as a fact. Moreover, if a candidate begins to practice while she is still in her own analysis, this is clearly preferable to starting a practice after an analysis that was purely formal and through which nothing was really accomplished in the direction of modifying the libidinal economy. The analyst who begins to practice while still in analysis may have already acquired some knowledge of the unconscious, sufficient enough to put her own desire on another level, meaning she may have been led to see some of the traps of narcissism. This may enable her to see into repressions and to undo them. So, we thought that it's better to just admit the fact, and accept someone who did some personal analytic work as being herself a practitioner, rather than denying the fact altogether.

Control, or what is also called supervision, is recommended because, however far you may have gone in your own analysis, you can't at the same time act as an analyst and see what you're doing. Supervision is the occasion offered to you so that you may "see," so to speak, the dynamics and even the logic of the psychoanalytic movement or dialectic. This you can't do with just a colleague or a friend, because of the part of narcissism that is ineliminatable and which always interferes in such relations. So, it is better to have it with an elder, in the sense of one who has more experience, and to pay for it. That makes it work, confirms its quality as a work.

Moreover, the fact of having been analyzed or even well analyzed may enable you to grasp the unconscious significations of your analysand's discourse or associations. But you still won't necessarily know exactly what to do with what you understand. So there's a difference between the knowledge that you collect in the process and the use of that knowledge, and here the control may have such quality on this point that you may learn something from it. For example, an analyst may be led to see some paradox in what was delivered to her as material, and she may then be led to a very good question, although she doesn't know what to do with her question. It may be sufficient just to tell her that this is precisely the question to put to her patient. It's a simple answer, but what she needed to be told. To add to this, the analyst may be deaf to some hot points, which may lead to a negative transference. So, indicating these points to her may be very helpful. And, if such moments of deafness are repeated, so much so that the analysis itself is in danger, or if the analysis degenerates into an operation of mutual seduction, then the analyst under supervision will be led to see the insufficiency of her own analysis, which may invite her to resume it. And this is one of the very big services supervision may provide for the beginning analyst.

Question: You were in supervision with Lacan. Would you say something about this experience? What was he like as a supervisor?

Generally Lacan never intervened between my patient and me. He would rather appreciate the analyst's work and express his appreciation if it was good. This generally had a double effect, on one hand encouraging the analyst and making him feel relaxed in his work, and on the other making him notice what was efficient in his style of proceeding in his work, that is, enabling him to see what analysis *is*. Needless to say, Lacan was always open to all your theoretical questions, insofar as they were brought in apropos of the material, meaning what is said and done in the session.

He sometimes intervened when the analyst simply missed the point. For example, I remember having an analysand who was an automobile mechanic, and in one session the fellow began a long speech about his boss's son, who had just visited the shop. My analysand's discourse was filled with the passion of extraordinary hate, to the point that he had all his attention fixed on the features of his boss's son, describing his face, his golden sleeve buttons, and so on, and at the end of this hate-filled outburst he said he felt deflated, as if he had just masturbated. In my meeting with Lacan, I was prone to explain this hate as something addressed to his brother and repeated with his boss's son. Lacan was impatient, and he showed it. He pointed to the meaning for me, which was the statement about masturbation. My explanation was beside the point, because it didn't take into consideration the fact of the reference to masturbation that had come at the end.

Once he pointed to what I had missed, I could see that the hate was not a matter of a simple repetition of the relation with some historical figure, but was mainly a structural relation with the alter ego, that is, it was rather an expression of the murderous dimension in the relation with a narcissistic figure, the alter ego. Because I didn't notice the part about masturbation, Lacan drew my attention to this detail, which was vital. That's what I mean by intervening when you miss the point.

By way of a souvenir, Lacan once expressed his surprise to me because, he said, I had acted as an analyst, in some particular situation, in a way that was exactly comparable to how he himself would have acted. As he could tell that I was very pleased with this rapprochement, he immediately added, "I'm telling you this because it poses a problem for me; I don't knowingly give you any indication as to how to behave, and still it's there." So, the pleasure I had initially taken in his remark was a tad attenuated.

Question: What points do you consider important in a control analysis?

My thought is that when I have someone in control, I take her as someone who is solely responsible for the operation she leads. Moreover, her own responsibility is secondary; the first responsibility belongs to her analysand. What I mean is that the analyst can only play with the cards that are delivered to her by her analysand. But the point is whether or not she knows how to play with the cards given to her. If she plays well, that is, if her acts are appropriate, or even if she misses some points here or there that have no strategic value, I don't intervene at all, no more than Lacan did with me. I may intervene in the moments when the analyst herself is embarrassed, but usually even then I don't tell her what to do. Often an analyst expresses herself by saying, "I don't know whether I should do this or that," in which case I may tell her that *this* is better than *that*. Insofar as I say something, however, I take it as my duty to explain the reason.

The cases where I actually intervene between the analyst and her patients are very rare. For example, in cases where the analyst is deaf to an unconscious culpability that is expressing itself in real acts, which are not only auto-punitive but which may be putting the analysand's life in danger, I may intervene strongly, because herein lies my responsibility as a supervisor. This is one of the reasons supervision is not only recommended or advised, but necessary. There are also cases where analysis may prove to be a big maneuver of seduction, say on the part of the analysand, but with which the analyst complies, so much is the *jouissance* she takes from it. If this state of things continues, I may go to the extreme of telling the analyst that this is no longer analysis, and she should stop it! As a matter of fact, this amounts to putting the analyst in front of her own responsibility, and it will free her to either take the step or not, if she is up to her responsibility or not.

Printed in the United States
by Baker & Taylor Publisher Services